Interactive Vocabulary Lessons

Word Meaning

By Marjorie Frank and Jill Norris

Incentive Publications, Inc.
Nashville, Tennessee

Illustrated by Kathleen Bullock
Cover by Debbie Weekly
Copyedited by Cary Grayson

ISBN 978-0-86530-656-1

1   2   3   4   5   6   7   8   9   10   14   13   12   11

Printed by Sheridan Books, Inc., Chelsea, Michigan • April 2011
www.incentivepublications.com

Table of Contents

About This Program

Word Meaning is a successful blend of high-tech and traditional classroom activities. The program includes a CD with a set of interactive digital whiteboard lessons to teach and practice vocabulary skills dealing with context, denotation and connotation, synonyms, and antonyms. In addition, this teacher guide provides print support of the same skills.

Each vocabulary skill is first introduced with an interactive *Learn It!* activity. These lessons include *Discuss It!* prompts. Following the introduction of a skill, students move through several interactive *Practice It!* activities to facilitate initial guided practice of the new skill. At the end of the unit on *Word Meaning*, interactive review activities encourage students to apply the skills they have just learned.

The teacher guide includes:

- tips for each interactive screen;

- valuable printable resources that support the interactive whiteboard activities: hints for finding meanings in context, hints for comparing denotation and connotation, common synonyms, common antonyms, and a glossary;

- a cumulative review and assessment; and

- eight pages of paper-pencil practice reinforcing the skills.

Navigating the Whiteboard Activities

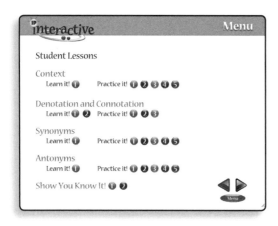

The Menu screen allows you to access any lesson or practice by touching its title.

Touch the Menu icon  on any screen to move back to this screen.

Use the forward and back arrows ◀ ▷ to move forward or backward one screen.

The reset icon allows you to clear work on a screen and restore it to its original look.

① ② ③ ④ ⑤ The numbers at the top of the screen indicate the number of *Learn It!* or *Practice It!* pages dealing with a specific skill. These numbers are active. Touch the number to move to that screen.

Print Support

Cumulative Review and Assessment

When the whole class, small groups, or individuals have completed the lessons, use the printable cumulative review and assessment to check students' understanding of the skills.

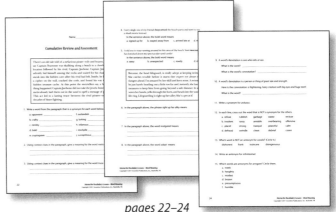

pages 22–24

Printable References

Imagine how handy it is to have printable references for students to refer to when they are away from the whiteboard lesson. The hints and lists are great additions to a vocabulary journal and will help students discover the meanings of words.

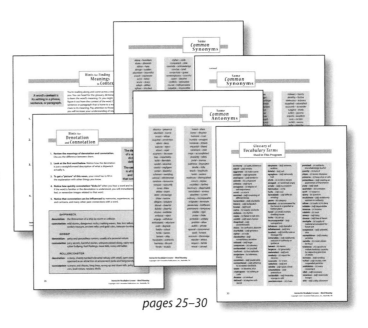

pages 25–30

Printable Practice Pages

Reinforce the skills taught in the interactive lessons with engaging paper-pencil practice activities. Each activity demands higher-level thinking and requires students to apply what they have learned.

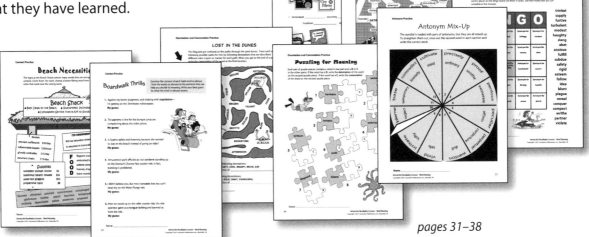

pages 31–38

Vocabulary Standards and Skills Supported by This Program

Standard-Skill	Screens (Sc) • Pages (Pg)
Use context to determine the meaning of a word	**Sc:** 4, 5, 8, 9 **Pg:** 25, 31, 32
Identify context clues that suggest the meaning of a particular word or phrase	**Sc:** 4, 5, 8 **Pg:** 25, 31, 32
Use context to choose the correct word for a particular situation	**Sc:** 6, 7, 8, 9 **Pg:** 25, 31, 32
Use context to determine the meaning of a phrase	**Pg:** 25, 32
Distinguish between denotation and connotation; identify situations in which each would be important	**Sc:** 10, 13, 14 **Pg:** 26, 33, 34
Describe the connotation of a word	**Sc:** 11, 12 **Pg:** 26, 33, 34
Recognize synonyms for a word	**Sc:** 15, 16, 17, 18, 19, 20, 27, 28 **Pg:** 27, 28, 35, 36, 38
Use synonyms to show understanding of word meaning	**Sc:** 15, 16, 17, 18, 19, 20, 27, 28 **Pg:** 27, 28, 35, 36, 38
Recognize antonyms for a word	**Sc:** 22, 23, 24, 25, 26, 27, 28 **Pg:** 29, 37, 38
Use antonyms to show understanding of word meaning	**Sc:** 22, 23, 24, 25, 26, 27, 28 **Pg:** 29, 37, 38

Common Core Curriculum 6–12 Anchor Standards Supported by This Program

Anchor Standards for	Number and Category	Standard
Reading	**4:** Craft and Structure	Interpret words and phrases as they are used in a text, including determining technical, connotative, and figurative meanings, and analyze how specific word choices shape meaning or tone
Speaking and Listening	**2:** Comprehension and Collaboration	Integrate and evaluate information presented in diverse media and formats, including visually, quantitatively, and orally
Language	**4:** Vocabulary Acquisition and Use	Determine or clarify the meaning of unknown and multiple-meaning words and phrases by using context clues, analyzing meaningful word parts, and consulting general and specialized reference materials, as appropriate
Language	**5:** Vocabulary Acquisition and Use	Demonstrate understanding of word relationships and nuances in word meanings

Thinking Skills Supported by This Program

Structure Based on Bloom's Taxonomy of Cognitive Development

Cognitive Domain Levels Simplest ➡ Most Complex	Skills	Screens (Sc) and Pages (Pg)
Remembering: Recall data or information	arrange, define, describe, duplicate, label, list, match, name, order, recall, recognize, repeat, reproduce, select, state	**Sc:** 4, 5, 6, 7, 8, 9, 10, 11, 12, 13, 14, 15, 16, 17, 18, 19, 20, 21, 22, 23, 24, 25, 26, 27, 28 **Pg:** 31, 32, 33, 34, 35, 36, 37, 38
Understanding: Understand the meaning, translation, interpolation, and interpretation of instructions and problems; explain concepts and state a problem in one's own words	classify, describe, discuss, explain, express, identify, indicate, locate, recognize, report, select, translate, paraphrase	**Sc:** 4, 5, 6, 7, 8, 9, 10, 11, 12, 14, 14, 15, 16, 17, 18, 19, 20, 21, 22, 23, 24, 25, 26, 27, 28 **Pg:** 31, 32, 33, 34, 35, 36, 37, 38
Applying: Use a concept in a new situation or unprompted use of an abstraction	apply, choose, demonstrate, dramatize, employ, illustrate, interpret, operate, practice, schedule, sketch, solve, use, write	**Sc:** 4, 5, 6, 7, 8, 9, 10, 11, 12, 13, 14, 15, 16, 17, 18, 19, 20, 21, 22, 23, 24, 25, 26, 27, 28 **Pg:** 31, 32, 33, 34, 35, 36, 37, 38
Analyzing: Distinguish among component parts to arrive at meaning or understanding	analyze, appraise, calculate, categorize, compare, contrast, criticize, differentiate, discriminate, distinguish, examine, experiment, question, test	**Sc:** 4, 5, 6, 7, 8, 9, 10, 11, 12, 16, 17, 18, 19, 20, 21, 22, 23, 24, 25, 26, 27, 28 **Pg:** 31, 32, 34, 35, 36, 37
Evaluating: Justify a decision or position; make judgments about the value of an idea	appraise, argue, assess, defend, evaluate, judge, rate, select, support, value, compose, construct, create, design, develop, formulate, manage, organize, plan, prepare, propose, set up, write	**Sc:** 4, 5, 6, 7, 8, 9, 10, 11, 12, 17, 18, 19, 20, 21, 25, 26 **Pg:** 31, 32, 33, 34, 35
Creating: Create a new product or viewpoint	assemble, construct, create, design, develop, formulate, mold, prepare, propose, synthesize, write	**Sc:** 21, 25, 26, 28 **Pg:** 31, 32, 34

Using Interactive Whiteboards in the Classroom

Interactive whiteboard activities help you capture student attention with content-rich, dynamic lessons, engaging your students in standards-based skill practice using hands-on activities that feel more like fun than work. Interactive whiteboards allow today's teachers to share ideas and information and to involve their students in learning with technology. Whiteboard activities offer shared learning experiences for large or small groups, as well as high-interest practice for individuals.

One-computer classrooms can maximize the use of limited computer access by using the whiteboard. Students work together with individuals contributing at the board, other participants at the computer, and the group as a whole discussing the activity. The participation that transpires between the person at the computer, the users at the board, and the computer itself is a unique and very adaptable arrangement.

Whiteboard activities accommodate different learning styles. Tactile learners benefit from touching and marking at the board, audio learners listen to audio prompts and class discussions, while visual learners can see what is taking place as it develops at the board.

Interactive whiteboards can be a helpful tool for differentiating learning. Learners have a large focal point and a colorful image that focuses their attention. The whiteboard motivates reluctant learners, but it also appeals to both higher- and lower-level learners.

Teachers easily integrate digital whiteboard instruction to meet standards requiring teaching with technology.

Tips for Getting Started

1) Choose the location of your interactive board carefully. Consider whether large windows will require blinds on a sunny day. Think about the height of viewers. Remember that a board and extra equipment can require as many as six nearby electric sockets.

2) If something doesn't work, don't be afraid to ask a student for help.

3) Take any training classes that are offered to you. Then adapt the recommendations to fit your classroom.

4) Don't limit interactive whiteboard use to whole-group presentations. It is a valuable tool for small-group instruction and individual practice.

5) Be sensitive to the middle-school student's fear of looking different and being wrong. Some students may prefer to work in teams.

6) Using digital video cameras, voting systems, and scanners with your whiteboard can take your lessons to very exciting places. Document cameras are extremely powerful when used with an interactive whiteboard. They project onto the board anything placed under them.

7) Record your instruction and post the material for review by students at a later time.

Screen-by-Screen Teacher Tips

Context

Denotation and Connotation

Synonyms

Antonyms

Synonyms and Antonyms

Screen-by-Screen Teacher Tips

Context   Learn It! 1

Ask students: *How do you figure out the meaning of a new word?*

You may want to list their responses. Recognize each valid response. If no one suggests that the words around the new word often hold clues to its meaning, introduce the term *context* and explain that together you will discover how the context of a word helps the reader understand what the word means.

Read the sentences at the top of the screen together and then investigate context in sentences and paragraphs by touching the cartoons to see and hear the messages in the talk bubbles.

Encourage students to use the context to determine the meanings of the two new words.

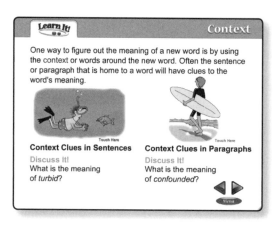

Context   Practice It! 1

Invite students to apply their understanding of context to determine the meaning of the blue words in the three sentences.

> largesse
> > clue: donating all the buckets
> > meaning: generosity

> paucity
> > clue: need several more
> > meaning: scarcity

> cajole
> > clue: reluctant to work
> > meaning: coax, persuade

After students have suggested meanings for the words, touch the pictures to confirm their ideas with audio definitions.

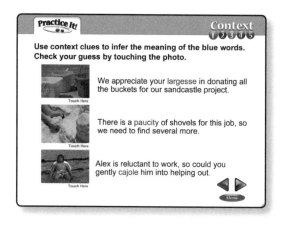

Context   Practice It! 2

In this activity students will be determining which verb fits the context of the sentence. Encourage them to explain why they select the words they do.

Drag the word chosen into the blank.
If it stays, it is the correct word.

> We need to **augment** this structure because we don't have enough sections in our sandcastle.

> Our tools are missing! Someone must have **absconded** with them.

> The castle must be just right, because the judges will **scrutinize** every inch of it.

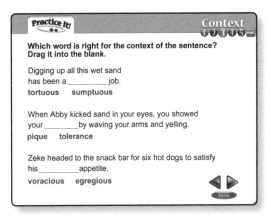

Context   Practice It! 3

Students analyze each sentence and choose the best adjective or noun to complete the sentence. Encourage them to explain why they select the words they do and to suggest the words' meaning.

When the correct word is dragged into the correct blank, it will stay.

> Digging up all this wet sand has been a **tortuous** job.

> When Abby kicked sand in your eyes, you showed your **pique** by waving your arms and yelling.

> Zeke headed to the snack bar for six hot dogs to satisfy his **voracious** appetite.

Context   Practice It! 4

Encourage students to identify clues in the passage that suggest the meaning of each correct word and analyze the meanings of the four choices.

> The word probably means *subdue* or *allay* (better weather, dying winds).

> *Encourage*, *incite*, and *aggravate* "stir up" the opposite image.

> Therefore, the correct answer must be *quell*.

Have them drag the words into the blanks to check their thinking.

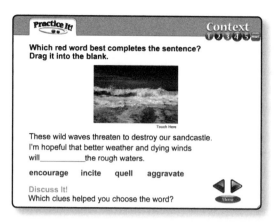

Context   Practice It! 5

Follow the procedure that students followed on the previous screen to analyze the sentences and choose the best word to complete each idea meaningfully.

Have students drag words into the blanks to check their reasoning.

> Have you ever floated on a raft and *been rocked to sleep* by the *gentle* **undulation** of the waves?

> The kelp forest is a busy community of **diverse** creatures that, *despite their differences*, live together harmoniously.

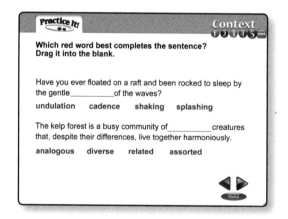

Denotation and Connotation   Learn It! 1

Introduce the terms *denotation* and *connotation*, or review the difference between the terms if your students already have been introduced to them.

The paragraph gives both the denotation and the connotation of *treasure*. Encourage students to personalize the connotation by thinking what images the word creates in their minds.

Touch the cartoon of the pirate to see and hear a second example of denotation and connotation in the talk bubble.

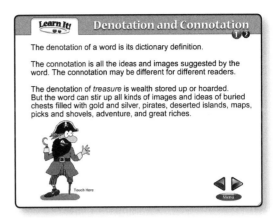

Denotation and Connotation   Learn It! 2

Touch number one, to see and hear the shipwrecked woman's initial response:

> I'm feeling *uneasy*.

Touch the remaining numbers in order, to escalate her response.

> I'm *terrified*.
>
> I'm *desperate*.
>
> I'm *panicked*.

Encourage students to discuss how the connotation of different similar-meaning words changes the intensity of a sentence.

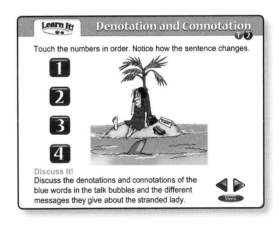

Denotation and Connotation
Practice It! 1

The pairs of sentences in this activity are identical except for a single word. Encourage children to recognize the change that the connotation of a word brings to the meaning of a sentence.

Have students touch the word that has the most extreme connotation in each pair.

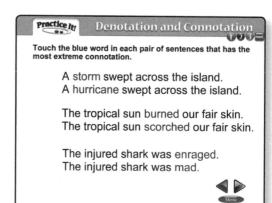

Denotation and Connotation
Practice It! 2

Students identify whether a given definition reflects the denotation or connotation of a word.

If the definition given represents the connotation of the word, encourage students to also state its denotation.

If the definition given represents the denotation of the word, encourage students to give its connotation.

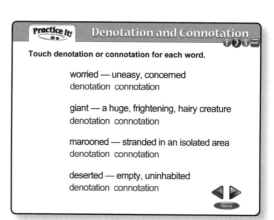

Denotation and Connotation
Practice It! 3

Students identify whether a given definition reflects the denotation or connotation of a word.

If the definition given represents the connotation of the word, encourage students to also state its denotation.

If the definition given represents the denotation of the word, encourage students to give its connotation.

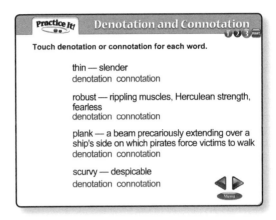

Synonyms   Learn It! 1

Introduce or review the term *synonyms*. Have students look at the photograph and suggest synonyms for *beach*. One example is given in the text, and three more appear when the seashells are touched.

Encourage students to create a list of additional synonyms.

(coast, seaside, shoreline, sand)

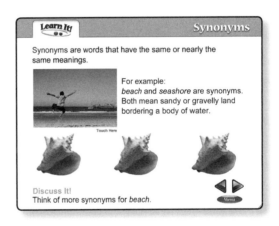

Synonyms   **Practice It! 1**

Challenge students to make synonym pairs with robust vocabulary words.

Students drag the words into place.

Encourage students to give the meaning of the synonyms.

cipher and cryptogram	(code, secret message)
adroit and nimble	(lively)
refuse and rubbish	(waste)
genre and category	(type, kind)

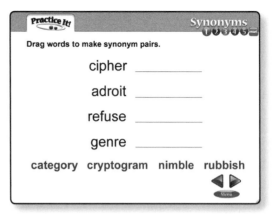

Synonyms   **Practice It! 2**

Continue with the same type of practice.

Encourage students to suggest a meaning for the synonym pairs.

cache and stockpile	(supply, store)
nefarious and infamous	(notorious)
intractable and recalcitrant	(stubborn)
composure and aplomb	(assurance)

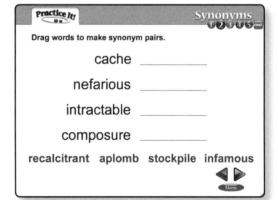

Synonyms   Practice It! 3

Challenge students to look at the three words in each row and to choose the one that is not a synonym of the other two. Students drag the "oddball" word into the net.

Encourage students to explain their decisions.

> I picked *brazen* because
> it means bold, not secretive.

> I picked *malevolent* because
> it means malicious, not charitable.

> I picked *facile* because
> it means simplistic, not difficult.

Synonyms   Practice It! 4

Invite students to choose the blue word that is a synonym of the italicized word in the sentence.

When the correct word is touched, a *Yes!* button will appear.

skittish   skulking   sullen

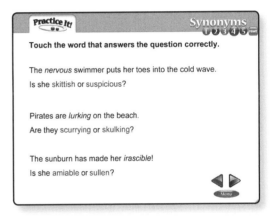

Synonyms   Practice It! 5

Students continue the practice activity from the previous screen. They will touch the blue word that is a synonym for the italicized word in the sentence.

sassy   surreptitious   uncomfortable

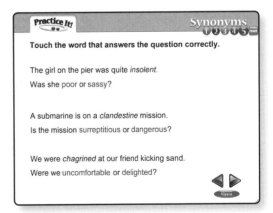

Antonyms   Learn It! 1

Introduce or review the term *antonyms*. Have students point out the example in the photograph.

Shivering is the opposite of scorching. Challenge students to think of more antonyms for scorching. Touch the shells to see three possibilities.

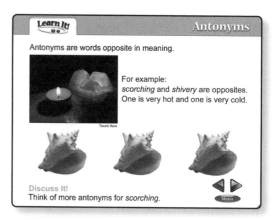

Antonyms   Practice It! 1

Encourage students to develop a plan for creating the antonym pairs.

Figure out the meaning of the first word. (*Candid* means *frank*.)

Think of the antonym of *frank* (*evasive*).

Read the words in the word bank and find one that could be a synonym for *evasive* (*wily*).

Drag the word from the word bank into the footprint.

candid — wily

infinitesimal — colossal

consistent — erratic

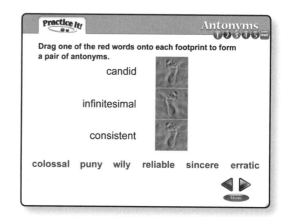

Antonyms   Practice It! 2

Follow the plan for identifying antonym pairs that you have developed for previous screens. Continue the practice activity from the previous page with three new sets of antonyms.

conjecture — proof

arrogance — modesty

fabrication — truth

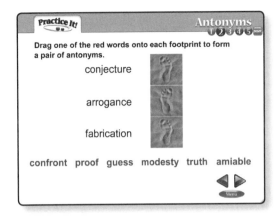

Antonyms   Practice It! 3

Continue the practice activity from the previous screen with three new sets of antonyms.

elude — confront

preserve — ruin

hovel — castle

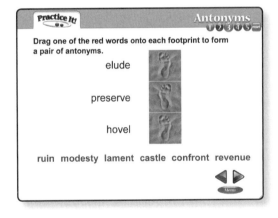

Antonyms   Practice It! 4

Invite students to read the first sign and to find a word that does not make sense in the context of the warning. *(There would not be a danger in placid or calm surf.)*

Once students have found the discrepancy, have them locate a word in the word bank that is the antonym of the problem word and drag the new word onto the sign.

Repeat for the second sign (*placate* should be *annoy*).

When students have fixed the signs, have them think of other words that would also have worked as replacements.

Antonyms   Practice It! 5

Continue the practice from the previous screen.

> nauseate — please
>
> public — private

Synonyms and Antonyms
Show You Know It! 1

Challenge students to review what they know by completing this chart including both synonyms and antonyms.

  inconsequential   (unimportant, vital)

  bizarre   (outlandish, conventional)

  pandemonium   (chaos, order)

  ostentatious   (pretentious, tasteful)

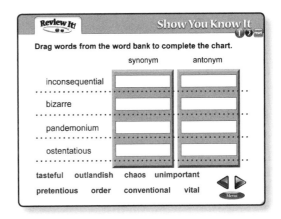

Synonyms and Antonyms
Show You Know It! 2

If your students are not familiar with analogies, take the time to analyze an example before beginning the screen. Remind students to examine the relationship of the two words that are shown on one side of the analogy.

  Deceive and *swindle* are synonyms, so students will need to find a synonym for *cozen*. (defraud)

  Doleful and *cheerful* are antonyms, so students will need to find an antonym for *certainty*. (quandary)

  Assail and *attack* are synonyms, so students will need to find a synonym for *savory*. (tasty)

Ask students to identify a difference between the two analogies where the relationship is synonyms. (In the first analogy, *cozen*, *defraud*, *deceive*, and *swindle* are all synonyms for each other. In the last analogy, there are two pairs of synonyms.)

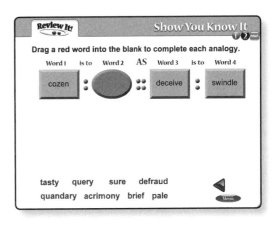

Cumulative Review and Assessment

There's an old tale told of a nefarious pirate—wily and brazen. They say Captain Fearsome was skulking along a beach to a clandestine location followed by his rival, Captain Jawbone. Captain Jawbone adroitly hid himself among the rocks and waited for his chance to sneak into the hidden cave after his rival had left. Inside, he found a cipher on the wall, cracked the code, and found his way to the hidden treasure cache. At this point the storytellers say, a bizarre thing happened. Captain Jawbone did not take the jewels. Instead, he meticulously laid them out in the sand to spell a message of peace. This act led to a lasting truce between the rival pirates—ending decades of bitter fighting.

1. Write a word from the paragraph that is a synonym for each word below.

   a. opponent _____ f. outlandish _____

   b. crafty _____ g. lurking _____

   c. nimbly _____ h. infamous _____

   d. bold _____ i. stockpile _____

   e. cryptogram _____ j. surreptitious _____

2. Using context clues in the paragraph, give a meaning for the word *meticulously*.

   _____

   _____

3. Using context clues in the paragraph, give a meaning for the word *truce*.

   _____

   _____

4. Every single one of my friends **boycotted** the beach party and went to see a shark movie instead.

    In the sentence above, the bold word means

    a. signed up for   b. stayed away from   c. arrived late at   d. made fun of

5. I told you to stop running around in this area of the beach. Your **raucous** behavior has knocked down my spectacular sand castle!

    In the sentence above, the bold word means

    a. sassy   b. unexpected   c. rowdy   d. mellow

Breanne, the head lifeguard, is really adept at keeping swimmers safe. She catches trouble before it starts—her expert eye always seeing the dangers ahead. I'm amazed by her skill and keen sense. A swimmer might be just barely heading out a little too far and, instantly, she has instigated measures to keep him from going beyond a safe distance. In a flash, she waves her hands, yells through the horn, and heads into the water with her life ring. Lifeguarding is right up her alley. She's a pro at it!

---

6. In the paragraph above, the phrase *right up her alley* means

    _____

    _____

7. In the paragraph above, the word *instigated* means

    _____

    _____

8. In the paragraph above, the word *adept* means

    _____

    _____

9. A word's denotation is *one who robs at sea.*

    What is the word? _____

    What is the word's connotation? _____

10. A word's denotation is *a person or thing of great size and strength.*

    Here is the connotation: *a frightening, hairy creature with big eyes and huge teeth*

    What is the word? _____

11. Write a synonym for *arduous.*

12. In each line, cross out the word that is NOT a synonym for the others.

    a. refuse   rubbish   garbage   waste   recluse

    b. insolent   sassy   amiable   overbearing   offensive

    c. placid   strong   tranquil   peaceful   calm

    d. defraud   swindle   cheat   debrief   cozen

13. Which word is NOT an antonym for *candid*? (Circle it.)

    dishonest   frank   insincere   disingenuous

14. Write an antonym for *infinitesimal.*

15. Which words are antonyms for *arrogant*? Circle them.

    a. meek
    b. haughty
    c. modest
    d. brazen
    e. presumptuous
    f. humble

Interactive Vocabulary Lessons—Word Meaning
Copyright ©2011 Incentive Publications, Inc., Nashville, TN

A word's **context** is its setting in a phrase, sentence, or paragraph.

You're reading along and come across a word that stumps you. You can head for the glossary, dictionary, or Internet to learn the word's meaning. Or, you might just be able to figure it out from the context of the word. Often the sentence or paragraph that is home to a word will have clues to its meaning. Pay attention to those clues, and you will increase your understanding of new words.

1. Look for clues in the text.

In this sentence, the phrases *muscular lifeguard* and *hauling in the waterlogged boat* suggest that **herculean** means *requiring great strength or effort*.

> Let's get that muscular lifeguard to help us with this **herculean** task of hauling in the waterlogged boat.

2. Look for pairs of words that might be antonyms to each other.

Paucity is associated with little food. *Plethora* is associated with plenty. You can figure out that **paucity** means *shortage* and **plethora** means *a lot!*

> Last year there was a **paucity** of food at the school beach party. I went home starved. This year, there is a **plethora** of delicious choices.

3. Figure out the part of speech from the word's context.

Trudged is preceded by a subject (We) and modified by an adverb (painfully). This tells that it is a verb. *Painfully*, *tangled thickets of seaweed*, and *weariness* give more clues that **trudged** means *walked heavily and slowly*.

> We **trudged** painfully through the tangled thickets of seaweed looking for the lost fishing rod—until we gave up from weariness.

4. Look for a familiar word that might be a synonym for the unknown word.

Frenetic waves is paired with *frantic cry*, suggesting that the two words might have similar meanings. Indeed, **frenetic** means *frantic*.

> With **frenetic** waves
> And a **frantic** cry
> I signaled the lifeguard
> When that shark came by.

Hints for Denotation and Connotation

> **The denotation** of a word is its dictionary definition.
>
> **The connotation** is all the ideas and images that come to mind.

1. **Review the meanings of denotation and connotation.** Discuss the difference between them.

2. **Look at the first word below.** Notice how the denotation is just a straightforward description of what a shipwreck actually is.

3. **To get a "picture" of this noun,** your mind has to fill in the explanation with other things you know.

4. **Notice how quickly connotation "kicks in"** when you hear a word and its denotation. If the word is familiar or the denotation is understood, you will immediately start to see, feel, or remember images related to that word.

5. **Notice that connotation can be influenced** by memories, experiences, stories, movies and cartoons, and many other past connections with a word.

SHIPWRECK

denotation: the destruction of a ship by storm or collision

connotation: wild storms, dangerous rocks, crashing waves, fear, lost sailors, skeletons, sunken treasure, ancient relics and gold coins, treasure-hunting divers

GOSSIP

denotation: petty and groundless rumors, usually of a personal nature

connotation: juicy secrets, harmful stories, whispers passed along, nasty text messages, cyber-bullying, hurt feelings, mean kids, nosey old ladies

ROLLERCOASTER

denotation: a steep, sharply banked elevated railway with small, open passenger cars operated as an attraction at amusement parks and fairgrounds

connotation: screams and shouts, long lines, racing up and down hills, jerky rattling cars, loud noises, nausea, thrills

---

26

abase – humiliate
abate – diminish
abhor – hate
abrupt – sudden
abundant – bountiful
acquit – exonerate
acrid – bitter
acute – sharp
adept – skilled
aghast – shocked
allege – claim
ally – partner
altercation – argument
amicable – agreeable
apathy – indifference
appraise – evaluate
arrogant – haughty
astonish – confound
audacious – bold
avarice – greed
averse – opposed
baffle – confuse
bauble – trinket
belief – conviction
berate – criticize
bias – prejudice
bizarre – weird
boast – brag
brazen – bold
brusque – abrupt
calamity – disaster
callow – immature
candid – honest
capitulate – surrender
casual – informal
cease – desist
chaos – disorder
chide – scold
churlish – grumpy

cipher – code
competent – able
concede – acknowledge
concise – brief
conjecture – guess
contemptuous – scornful
cozen – deceive
credible – believable
crucial – indispensable
culpable – responsible
cunning – guile
dearth – shortage
debacle – disaster
dejected – disheartened
depleted – empty
deride – ridicule
dire – extreme
dishonest – duplicitous
disparage – discredit
dispute – feud
distress – anguish
divergent – different
divulge – reveal
docile – submissive
doleful – sad
durable – lasting
elude – escape
embellish – elaborate
eminent – famous
emulate – imitate
enchant – captivate
enmity – hatred
ensue – follow
erudite – scholarly
escapade – adventure
fabrication – lie
facile – free
falseness – duplicity
fervor – passion

forced – compelled
fortunate – auspicious
fraud – hoax
frenetic – frantic
frugal – prudent
furtive – sneaky
fury – rage
futile – ineffective
garbled – jumbled
generous – benevolent
genuine – real
goad – provoke
greed – avarice
grouchy – cranky
grueling – exhausting
guarantee – assure
gullible – unsuspicious
harass – annoy
haughty – arrogant
hazard – danger
hoist – raise
hoodlum – gangster
hoodwink – deceive
huge – immense
illicit – illegal
illusory – imaginative
imitate – copy
impeccable – flawless
implausible – unlikely
implicate – accuse
inadvertent – accidental
inane – silly
incensed – outraged
indelible – permanent
inept – incompetent
infamous – shameful
infirmity – sickness
inkling – idea
insolent – disrespectful

(continued)

(continued)

Some *Common* Synonyms

instigate – start	pallid – pale	stalwart – hearty
irritable – irascible	peril – danger	stealthy – furtive
irritate – annoy	perpetuate – continue	strenuous – arduous
jargon – slang	perplex – astonish	stupefied – astonished
jocose – playful	petulant – impatient	succumb – surrender
justification – excuse	phobia – fear	suggest – imply
languid – listless	pilfer – steal	sullen – gloomy
lavish – lush	pique – annoy	superb – excellent
lazy – indolent	placid – tranquil	sure – certain
lethal – fatal	plethora – excess	surfeit – excess
loathe – hate	poised – self-confident	surly – grouchy
lurid – sensational	predicament – dilemma	suspicious – skeptical
macabre – gruesome	promise – assurance	tame – subdue
malevolent – evil	pulverize – crush	tawdry – cheap
mandatory – required	quandary – doubt	tedium – boredom
mariner – sailor	query – question	tenuous – flimsy
mediocre – ordinary	quibble – argue	thwart – oppose
merge – blend	rampant – widespread	timorous – shy
miniscule – tiny	rebuff – reject	toil – labor
morose – gloomy	rebuke – scold	traditional – customary
murky – cloudy	recede – lessen	trivial – unimportant
mutual – joint	regime – administration	turbulent – stormy
notion – idea	reliable – dependable	unavoidable – inevitable
notorious – famous	repulsive – loathsome	unbelief – skepticism
novel – new	requisite – required	unscathed – unhurt
novice – beginner	response – answer	unseemly – indecent
noxious – harmful	reticent – shy	urbane – refined
obey – comply	rowdy – boisterous	vacillate – fluctuate
obstinate – stubborn	rude – insolent	vacuous – empty
obstreperous – stubborn	rupture – break	vagabond – wanderer
obstruct – impede	sagacity – wisdom	valid – legitimate
obtuse – blunt	sallow – pale	veritable – true
occurrence – instance	savory – tasty	vex – plague
omen – premonition	sedate – calm	vigorous – energetic
onus – blame	severed – cut	vulgar – gross
opponent – competitor	significant – important	wane – lessen
ostentations – showy	skulk – hide	writhe – squirm
outraged – exasperated	snarl – growl	yearly – annual
pacify – appease	squalid – filthy	zenith – top

absence – presence
abundant – scarce
accept – refuse
acquittal – conviction
admit – deny
approve – reject
attract – repel
augment – decrease
bias – impartiality
build – demolish
candid – secretive
careful – negligent
certain – doubtful
coherent – rambling
colossal – infinitesimal
condone – denounce
conquer – succumb
curse – bless
delete – insert
deter – encourage
dilate – narrow
diligent – indolent
dismal – cheerful
doleful – cheerful
elusive – available
embrace – reject
engage – withdraw
enthusiastic – reluctant
exalt – degrade
feeble – robust
fertile – barren
foment – allay
fraudulent – authentic
harmony – discord
hinder – enable

hoard – share
honor – disgrace
humane – cruel
humble – arrogant
immense – minute
impartial – biased
inclement – mild
inept – accomplished
jeopardy – safety
jovial – morose
judicious – imprudent
kindle – stifle
knack – ineptitude
lavish – austere
mediocre – distinguished
mourn – rejoice
muddled – clarified
necessary – dispensable
nonchalant – anxious
obsolete – current
ordinary – incomparable
originate – terminate
passionate – indifferent
permanent – temporary
pliable – rigid
praise – chide
probable – unlikely
prohibit – allow
public – private
quarrel – concurrence
quell – foment
reassure – discourage
repulse – attract
respect – deride
reveal – conceal

sallow – ruddy
sanguine – pessimistic
scant – abundant
scorn – esteem
scrupulous – dishonest
sedate – agitate
shackle – free
shirk – fulfill
sincerity – deceit
slacken – accelerate
solace – pain
stationary – movable
synthesize – analyze
temporal – eternal
thrive – languish
thwart – abet
timely – inopportune
tolerant – prejudiced
tranquil – tempestuous
transitory – enduring
transparent – opaque
truth – fallacy
turbulent – placid
uncanny – ordinary
unforeseen – anticipated
unsavory – agreeable
vague – clear
vintage – modern
weakness – vigor
wily – candid
wisdom – folly
wise – imprudent
yen – loathing
yield – oppose
zealous – dispassionate

Glossary of
Vocabulary Terms
Used in This Program

acrimony – *(n)* spite, bitterness

adroit – *(adj)* nimble

aggravate – *(v)* make worse

amiable – *(adj)* agreeable

analogous – *(adj)* similar to

aplomb – *(n)* composure

arduous – *(adj)* hard

arrogance – *(n)* display of self-importance

assail – *(v)* attack

assorted – *(adj)* consisting of different kinds

benevolent – *(adj)* charitable

bizarre – *(adj)* outlandish

brazen – *(adj)* bold

cache – *(n)* supply; stockpile

cadence – *(n)* rhythm

cajole – *(v)* flatter or talk into

candid – *(adj)* open, honest

chagrined – *(adj)* uncomfortable

chaos – *(n)* confusion, disorder

charitable – *(adj)* generous

cipher – *(n)* code

clandestine – *(adj)* surreptitious, secretive

colossal – *(adj)* huge

composure – *(n)* calmness

confounded – *(v)* puzzled

confront – *(v)* face defiantly

conjecture – *(n)* inference, theory

consistent – *(adj)* predictable

conventional – *(adj)* adhering to accepted standards

cozen – *(v)* deceive, trick

cryptogram – *(n)* writing in code

deceive – *(v)* mislead

defraud – *(v)* deprive with deceit

desperate – *(adj)* extreme, reckless

doleful – *(adj)* sad

egregious – *(adj)* extremely bad

elude – *(v)* avoid or escape

enraged – *(v)* extremely angry

erratic – *(adj)* inconsistent

fabrication – *(n)* lie

facile – *(adj)* easy

formidable – *(adj)* difficult; amazing

genre – *(n)* category

hoarded – *(v)* accumulated for the future in a guarded or hidden place

hovel – *(n)* small, humble dwelling house

incite – *(n)* stir up

inconsequential – *(adj)* unimportant

infamous – *(adj)* shameful

infinitesimal – *(adj)* tiny

insolent – *(adj)* boldly rude or disrespectful

intractable – *(adj)* stubbornly resistant to authority or guidance

lament – *(v)* mourn

largesse – *(n)* generosity

malevolent – *(adj)* evil

modesty – *(n)* regard for decency

nauseate – *(v)* sicken

nefarious – *(adj)* evil

nimble – *(adj)* quick; clever

ostentatious – *(adj)* pretentious

outlandish – *(adj)* freakishly strange or odd

pandemonium – *(n)* chaos

panicked – *(v)* suddenly, overwhelmingly fearful

paucity – *(n)* lack of

pique – *(v)* annoy; displease

preserve – *(v)* keep alive or safe

pretentious – *(adj)* creating an appearance of importance

puny – *(adj)* weak

quandary – *(n)* confusion

quell – *(v)* suppress

query – *(n)* question

recalcitrant – *(adj)* stubbornly resistant to authority

refuse – *(n)* trash; *(v)* to deny

reliable – *(adj)* dependable

revenue – *(n)* income

rubbish – *(n)* trash

savory – *(adj)* tasty

sincere – *(adj)* free of deceit

stockpile – *(n)* supply of material accumulated for future use

sumptuous – *(adj)* splendid, nice

surreptitious – *(adj)* sneaky; secretive

swindle – *(v)* cheat, obtain by fraud

tolerance – *(n)* capacity to endure hardship; capacity for respecting practices of others

tortuous – *(adj)* winding

turbid – *(adj)* muddy, with suspended particles

undulation – *(n)* wavy movement

vital – *(adj)* necessary

voracious – *(adj)* ravenously hungry

wily – *(adj)* crafty; dishonest

Beach Necessities

The signs at the Beach Shack contain many words that are not quite right for their context. Circle them. For each, choose a better-fitting word from the list below and write that word near the wrong word.

Beach Shack

- Best Deals on the Beach
- Guaranteed, Inconsequential Prices
- Complacent Service from 8 AM to Sundown

Rentals

relevant surfboards	$30/day
inflammable kayaks	$20/hour
ghastly umbrellas	$15/day
recurrent chairs	$15/day

$30 EQUIPMENT DEPOSIT

Will be refunded when equipment is returned in honorable condition

F O O D

flagrant snow cones	$2
embroiled hot dogs	$5
palette-pleasing pizza	$3
homely chips	$1
bone-numbing drinks	$1

Supplies

nonslimy suntan lotion	$2
luminous beach towels	$12
asserted goggles	$10
projective hats	$8

flavored · chivalrous · assorted · conscientious · undamaged · nongreasy · gigantic · homemade · inflatable · gluttonous · broiled · placid · luxurious · protective · proposed · thrifty · chilled · reclining · dependable · palate

Boardwalk Thrills

Examine the context of each bold word or phrase. Circle the words or phrases in the sentence that can help you decide its meaning. Write your best guess for what the word or phrase means.

1. Against my better judgment, and shaking with **trepidation**— I'm getting on the *Terminator* rollercoaster.
   My guess:

2. The **patrons** in line for the bungee jump are complaining about the ticket prices.
   My guess:

3. Is Sophia **sullen** and frowning because she wanted to stay on the beach instead of going on rides?
   My guess:

4. Amusement park officials do not **condone** standing up on the Stomach Churner fast coaster ride. In fact, standing is prohibited.
   My guess:

5. I didn't believe you. But now I **concede** that you can't keep dry on the *Water Plunge* ride.
   My guess:

6. After we stood up on the roller coaster ride, the ride operator **gave us a tongue-lashing** and banned us from the ride.
   My guess:

Name _____

Denotation and Connotation Practice

LOST IN THE DUNES

The lifeguard got confused on the paths through the sand dunes. Trace each of the following possible paths for him by following denotations that are described. Use a different color crayon or marker for each path. When you get to the end of a path, write the connotation of the word at the final location.

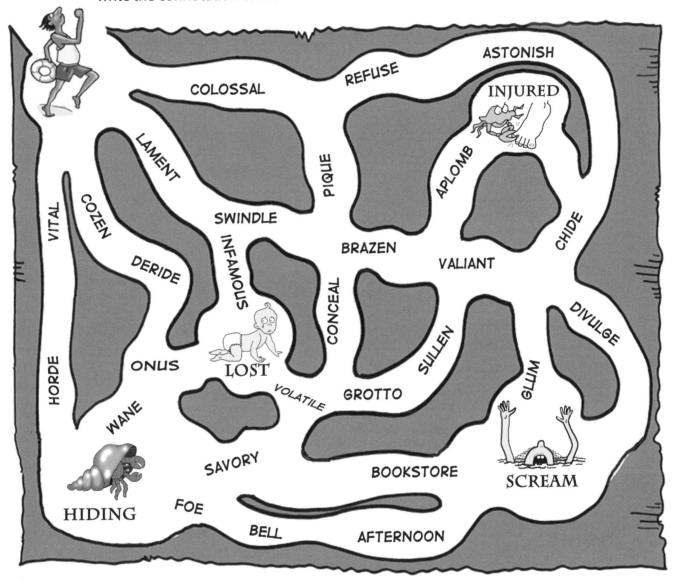

1. If he follows a path with words having the following denotations:

   NECESSARY, MOB, SHRINK, ENEMY, TASTY, CAVE, GRUMPY, BRAVE, SAD

   he will end up at a location with a connotation of _____

2. If he follows a path words having the following denotations:

   HUGE, TRASH, AMAZE, SCOLD, BRAVE, BOLD, CHEAT, DISGRACEFUL

   he will end up at a location with a connotation of _____

Name _____

Puzzling for Meaning

Each pair of puzzle pieces contains a word in one part and a **D** or **C** in the other piece. If the word has a **D**, write the **denotation** of the word on the second puzzle piece. If the word has a **C**, write the **connotation** of the word on the second puzzle piece.

1 hurricane C

2 anchor D

3 octopus D

4 undertow C

5 sunburn C

6 yacht C

7 lifeguard D

8 bizarre D

Name _____

TITLE PUZZLERS

In the rows of CDs, find one synonym on a CD
cover to match each word written below the row.

1. terminated _____ occurring _____ envisioning _____

    hoodlum _____ discarded _____

2. agony _____ sauntering _____ confusion _____

    scarcity _____ discourse _____

3. ambivalent _____ residual _____ baffled _____

Name _____

SYNONYM SEARCH

This underwater path is scattered with barriers. Move through them by finding one or more synonyms of the bold word in a circle. When you hit the next circle, find one or more synonyms of that word to continue on the path. Follow one right path that will break the barriers and take you back to the starting point.

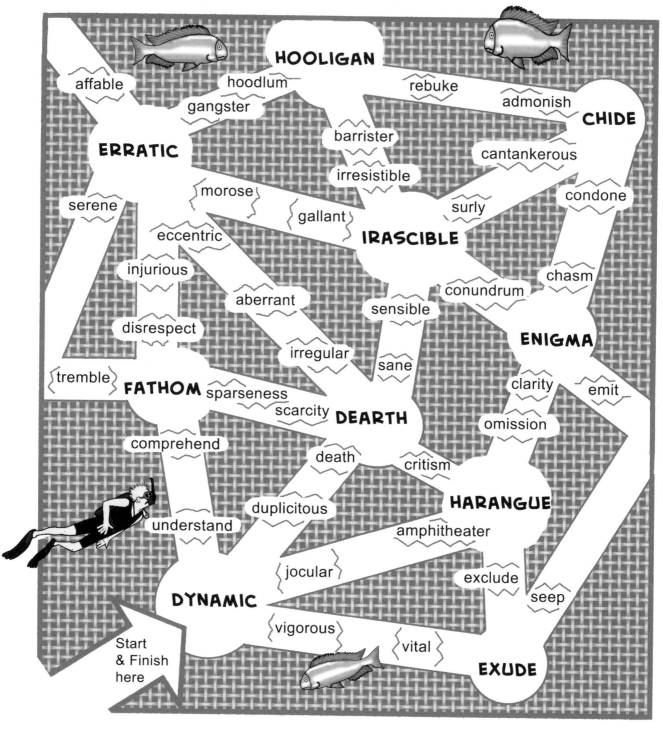

Name _____

Antonym Mix-Up

The sundial is loaded with pairs of antonyms, but they are all mixed up.
To straighten them out, cross out the second word in each section and
write the correct word.

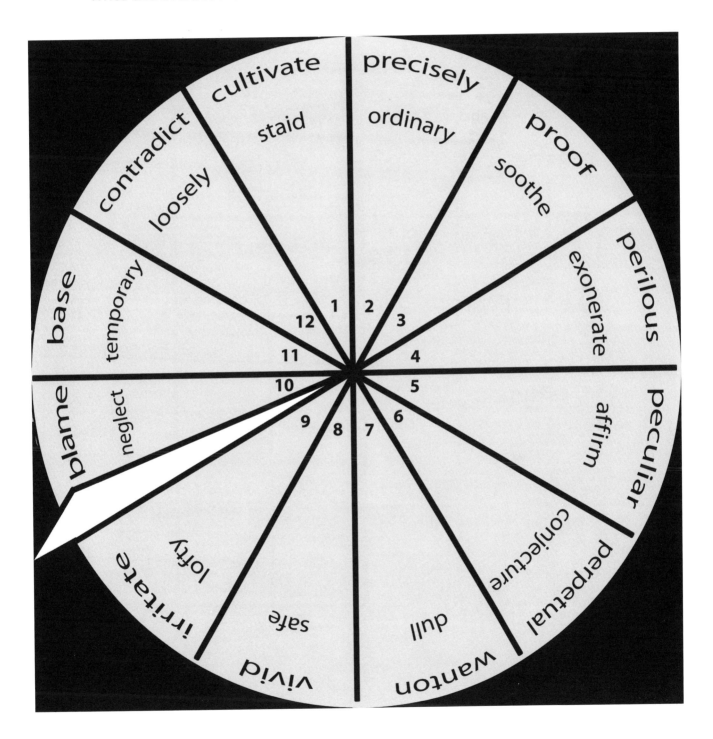

BINGO BEFORE THE BUZZER

Set a buzzer or other timer for five minutes. Write the words from the side into their correct places on the bingo board. Do them in order. See how many rows you can complete in five minutes.

B	I	N	G	O
Synonym for dense	Antonym for deprive	Synonym for regard	Synonym for infringe	Synonym for insolent
Synonym for jargon	Synonym for tame	Synonym for obtuse	Synonym for sneaky	Antonym for shirk
Synonym for vex	Antonym for vain	YOU WRITE a Synonym for TERRIFIC	Antonym for nonchalant	Synonym for squirm
Antonym for jeopardy	Synonym for inkling	Antonym for thwart	Synonym for divulge	Synonym for bauble
Synonym for ally	Antonym for pliable	Antonym for succumb	Synonym for ensue	Antonym for placid

trinket
supply
furtive
turbulent
modest
haughty
slang
abet
anxious
fulfill
subdue
safety
rigid
esteem
follow
idea
blunt
plague
reveal
conquer
compact
writhe
partner
violate

Name _____

Interactive Vocabulary Lessons—Word Meaning
Copyright ©2011 INCENTIVE PUBLICATIONS, Inc., Nashville, TN

Answer Key

Cumulative Review and Assessment, pages 22–24

1. a. rival
    b. wily
    c. adroitly
    d. brazen
    e. cipher
    f. bizarre
    g. skulking
    h. nefarious
    i. cache
    j. clandestine
2. Answers will vary. (Definition: precisely, carefully)
3. Answers will vary. (Definition: armistice, agreement to stop hostilities)
4. b
5. c
6. Answers will vary. (She's just right for this. OR She's really good at lifeguarding.)
7. Answers will vary. (Definition: started or initiated)
8. Answers will vary. (Definition: skilled, proficient)
9. pirate; Connotations will vary.
10. giant
11. Answers will vary. (difficult, laborious)
12. a. recluse; b. amiable; c. strong; d. debrief
13. frank
14. Answers will vary. (Definition: tiny)
15. a, c, f

Paper and Pencil Practice, pages 31–38

p. 31

Beach Shack—Replace *inconsequential* with *thrifty*; *complacent* with *conscientious*

Rentals—Replace *relevant* with *dependable*; *inflammable* with *inflatable*; *ghastly* with *gigantic*; *recurrent* with *reclining*

Deposit Sign—Replace *honorable* with *undamaged*

Food—Replace *flagrant* with *flavored*; *embroiled* with *broiled*; *palette* with *palate*; *homely* with *homemade*; *bone-numbing* with *chilled*

Supplies—Replace *nonslimy* with *nongreasy*; *luminous* with *luxurious*; *asserted* with *assorted*; *projective* with *protective*

p. 32

Student guesses should be similar to the actual meanings. The clues they circle should be sensible hints to the word meaning.

1. fear or apprehension
2. customers
3. sad, grumpy
4. permit, approve
5. eventually agree
6. scolded us

p. 33

1. This path will include the following words: vital, horde, wane, foe, savory, grotto, sullen, valiant, glum and will end with a connotation for SCREAM. (Student connotations will differ.)
2. This path will include the following words: colossal, refuse, astonish, chide, valiant, brazen, swindle, infamous, and will end with a connotation for LOST. (Student connotations will differ.)

p. 34

1. hurricane.........Connotations will differ.
2. anchor..............D
3. octopus ....D
4. undertow........Connotations will differ.
5. sunburn...........Connotations will differ.
6. yacht.................Connotations will differ.
7. lifeguard..........D
8. bizarre..............D

p. 35

1. over, happening, seeing, gangster, dumped
2. heartbreak, walking, pandemonium, dearth, talk
3. undecided, leftover, mystified

p. 36

Path begins at START and follows these words:
DYNAMIC—vigorous—vital—
EXUDE—seep—emit—
ENIGMA—conundrum—
IRASCIBLE—surly—cantankerous—
CHIDE—admonish—rebuke—
HOOLIGAN—hoodlum—gangster—
ERRATIC—eccentric—aberrant—irregular—
DEARTH—scarcity—sparseness—
FATHOM—comprehend—understand—
back to DYNAMIC

p. 37

1. cultivate	neglect
2. precisely	loosely
3. proof	conjecture
4. perilous	safe
5. peculiar	ordinary
6. perpetual	temporary
7. wanton	staid
8. vivid	dull
9. irritate	soothe
10. blame	exonerate
11. base	lofty
12. contradict	affirm

p. 38

Row 1 across: compact, supply, esteem, violate, haughty
Row 2 across: slang, subdue, blunt, furtive, fulfill
Row 3 across: plague, modest, student synonyms for terrific will vary, anxious, writhe
Row 4 across: safety, idea, abet, reveal, trinket
Row 5 across: partner, rigid, conquer, follow, turbulent

Make your vocabulary instruction come alive with interactive whiteboard lessons that teach important skills and capture your students' attention. Contact Incentive Publications for information about the three other Interactive Whiteboard products in this Vocabulary Series:

www.IPinteractive.com

Confusing Words

Word Structure

Words to Know